Contents

Introduction

Treat your feet with this inspiring selection of fun and practical toe-warmers. A hand-knitted sock is a pleasure to own and will always outlive its commercially produced poor relation. Make them for yourself or as a unique gift for a treasured friend.

If you have mastered the basics of knitting and are ready for a new challenge, you'll find these socks for all ages and occasions fun and easy to make; every project is accompanied by clear instructions describing how to achieve perfect results. In addition, a techniques section explains all the essential skills, including how to turn heels and knit in the round. Quick to knit, these designs are an ideal way of using up oddments of yarn and make perfect portable projects for knitters on the go. We're sure you'll enjoy making them.

Buttoned slouch

These cosy fun socks are made from alpaca, which is wonderful to work with and divine to wear. Buy beautiful buttons to fasten these sexy slouches.

SIZE
- To suit ankle circumference 10in (25.5cm)
- Heel to toe 7½in (19cm) adjustable
- Heel to cuff 7in (18cm)

TENSION
- 10 sts and 14 rows to 4in (10cm) over st st on
- 4mm needles, using yarn double throughout
- Use larger or smaller needles to achieve correct tension

MATERIALS AND EQUIPMENT
- Garnstudio Drops Alpaca (180m per 50g) or any 4-ply alpaca yarn
- 4 x 50g balls
- Set of 4mm (UK8:US6) double-pointed needles
- 12 small buttons

SPECIAL TECHNIQUES
- Raised increase
- Wrapped stitches
- Cables
- Kitchener grafting

METHOD
Using yarn double throughout, cast on 56 sts.
Divide sts evenly between needles (14 sts on each needle).
Work 16 rounds k.
Round 17 (cable): K sts on N1 and N2; on N3 C4F k10, k sts on N4.
Rounds 18-22: K.
Round 23: Reverse cable by working C4B, k all other sts.
Still using double pointed needles, begin to work back and forth in rows.
At the same time, work a buttonhole (see below) in every 6th row.

Note: buttonholes will be formed on N1 and button band on N4.

Next row: K across sts on N1, N2 and N3 and on N4 k10, p4 sts.

Cont as set until 39 rows have been worked from start of sock.

BUTTONHOLE ROUND
K2, yo, k2tog.

SHAPE HEEL
Note: the heel is worked using short row shaping over the centre 28 sts, leaving the stitches not being worked on spare needles.

Row 1: (RS facing) k28, wrap 1, turn.
Row 2: P27, wrap 1, turn.
Rep rows 1 and 2 until 11 sts rem.
Next row: K11, pick up and k wrapped st, replace on left needle, turn.
Next row: P11, pick up and p wrapped st, replace on left needle, turn.
Next row: K12 pick up and k wrapped st, replace on left needle, turn.

Next row: P12 pick up and p wrapped st, replace on left needle, turn.

Rep as set by last 4 rows until all 28 centre sts are back on needles.

Cont on all 56 sts until 6 buttonholes have been worked.

Work 5 rounds st st.

Rearrange sts on 3 needles ready to return to circular knitting (14 sts on N1, 28 sts on N2, 14 sts on N3).

Next round: Cable 4 sts by transferring first 4 sts from N1 to cable needle and holding at front of work so they overlap the g-st button band, k to end of round, then k last 4 sts from N3 to N1.

Cont working in rounds until sock is 2in (5cm) shorter than length required to toe.

SHAPE TOE

Next round: K to last 3 sts on N1, k2tog, k1, on N2 k1, ssk, k to end, on N3 k to last 3 sts, k2tog, k1, on N4 k1, ssk, k to to end. Work in rounds, cont to dec as set.

Round 6: Reverse cable by slipping 4 sts on to cable needle and holding at back of work, k4, complete round foll decs as set. Cont to dec as set until 16 sts rem.

Graft sts together using Kitchener stitch.

SECOND SOCK

Complete to match first sock, reversing cables and positions of button and buttonhole band if desired so there are 'left' and 'right' socks.

MAKING UP

Press lightly.

Weave in any loose ends.

Sew on buttons to correspond with buttonholes.

Lacy knee-highs

These fabulous socks are playful yet warm. The beautiful colouring of the yarn is shown to advantage in the cable and lace pattern that extends over the top of the foot.

SIZE
- To fit medium adult woman

TENSION
- 24 sts and 38 rows to 4in (10cm) over stocking stitch using 3.25mm needles

MATERIALS AND EQUIPMENT
- Colinette Jitterbug Merino (291yd/267m per 100g hank)
- 4 x 100g hanks
- Set of 3.75mm (UK9:US5) double-pointed needles
- Set of 3.50mm (UK9–10:US4) double-pointed needles
- Set of 3.25mm (UK10:US3) double-pointed needles
Use larger or smaller needles to achieve correct tension.

NOTE
Two slightly different shades of this lovely variegated yarn are shown in the main images.

LEG
Using 3.75mm needles, cast on 50 sts and work 2 patt reps (16 rounds).
Change to 3.5mm needles and work 3 patt reps (24 rounds).
Change to 3.25mm needles and work 10 patt reps (80 rounds).

CABLE AND LACE PATTERN
Round 1: K2, p2, k2tog, yo, p2, k4, p2 k2tog, yo, p2, k2, p1, k1, p4, k2, p2, k2tog, yo, p2, k4, p2, k2tog, yo, p2, k2, p4.
Round 2 and all even rounds: Knit the knit sts and purl the purl sts.
Round 3: K2, p2, yo, ssk, p2, k4, p2 yo, ssk, p2, k2, p1, k1, p4, k2, p2, yo ssk, p2, k4, p2, k2tog, yo, p2, k2, p4.
Round 5: As round 1.
Round 7: K2, p2, yo, ssk, p2, k4, p2, k2tog, yo, p2, k2, p1, k1, p4, k2, p2, yo, ssk, p2, k4, p2, yo, ssk, p2, k2, p4.
Round 8: As round 2.

HEEL FLAP
Work 25 rows on N2 (25 sts) to form heel.

TURN HEEL
Row 1: K15, skpo, k1, turn.
Row 2: Sl1, p5, p2tog, turn.
Row 3: Sl1, k6, skpo, k1, turn.
Row 4: Sl1, p7, p2tog, turn.
Row 5: Sl1, k8, skpo, k1, turn.
Row 6: Sl1, p9, p2tog, turn.
Cont as above until 16 sts rem.

GUSSET
Knit stitches, but do not turn. Using N1, pick up and k 16 sts along each side of

heel flap, pick up and p1 st in the gap between heel flap and N2 (33 sts); using N2, k 26 sts for instep; using N3, pick up and k1 st in the gap between instep sts and heel flap, 16 sts along the side of the heel flap, and 8 sts from the heel. You should have a total of 84 sts (N1 33sts; N2 26 sts; N3 25 sts).

Round 1: Work to 3 sts from end of N1, k2 tog, k1; on N2, cont in cable pattern purling the rem sts; on N3 k1, ssk, work to end.
Round 2: Keeping cable and purl panel correct as set, k rem sts.
Rep these 2 rounds until 50 sts rem (12 sts on N1, 13 sts on N2 and 25 sts on N3).

FOOT
Purling top of foot and continuing cable pattern, work until foot measures 2in (5cm) less than length required. Divide sts evenly between 4 needles for dec round.
Next round: On N1 k to last 3 sts, k2 tog, k1; on N2 k1, skpo, cont in cable pattern; on N3 k to last 2 sts, k2tog, k1; on N4 k1, skpo, k to end.
Work as above, alternating dec/non-dec rounds until 32 sts rem.
Work every round as a dec round until 8 sts rem.

MAKING UP
Graft stitches together using Kitchener stitch. Press lightly.

City stripe

These colourful socks add a touch of fun to a sober business suit and can be worked in his favourite shades. They have a comfortable rounded toe and the heel is great to work.

SIZE
• To fit ankle circumference 8½in (22cm) mf
• Heel to toe 9in (23cm)

TENSION
• 32 sts to 10cm measured over Fair Isle pattern
• using 3mm needles

MATERIALS AND EQUIPMENT
• Cygnet 4 ply 75% wool/ 25% nylon (205m per 50g ball)
• 2 x 50g balls Black (M)
• 2 x 50g balls Fuchsia (C)
• Set of 3mm (UK11:US2–3) double-pointed needles

SPECIAL TECHNIQUES
Fair Isle

METHOD

Using M, cast on 64 sts divided between 3 needles (21 sts on N1; 21 sts on N2; 22 sts on N3).

Join, taking care not to twist sts.

Work 5 rounds k1, p1 rib.

Work 7 rounds k.

Join in C and work in colour patt throughout (see chart overleaf).

Work straight in patt until leg measures 4½in (11.5cm).

Divide stitches so there are 32 sts on heel needle and 16 sts on each instep needle.

SHAPE HEEL

Work on 32 heel sts in M only and in st st for 3 in (7.5cm) ending with a purl row.

Next row: K18, skpo, turn.

Next row: Sl1, p4, p2tog, turn.

Next row: Sl1, k5, skpo, turn.

Next row: Sl1, p6, p2tog, turn.

Cont in this way, working 1 st more on every row until there are 18 sts being worked on the needle.

Next row: k18, pick up 15 sts along side of heel; work across instep needle; using N3 pick up 15 sts along side of heel; k9 from the heel needle on to this needle. There should now be 24 sts on each heel needle and 32 sts on the instep needle.

Next round: Working from division in centre of heel, work to last 3 sts on next needle, k2 tog, k1, work across instep, on N3 k1, skpo, work to end of needle.

Next round: Work, keeping upper foot patt correct as set.

Rep these last 2 rounds until there are 16 sts on each heel needle.

Working sole in 2 x 2 Fair Isle (see chart overleaf) and upper foot in Fair Isle as set, work straight until foot measures 8½in (21.5cm) from back of heel, allowing 2½in (6.5cm) for toe.

SHAPE TOE

Round 1: Using M, on N1 k to last 3 sts, k2 tog, k1; on instep needle, k1, skpo, k to last 3 sts, k2 tog, k1; on N3 k1, skpo, k to end of needle.

Round 2: Using M, k.
Rep these 2 rounds until 16 sts rem.

MAKING UP

Graft rem sts together.

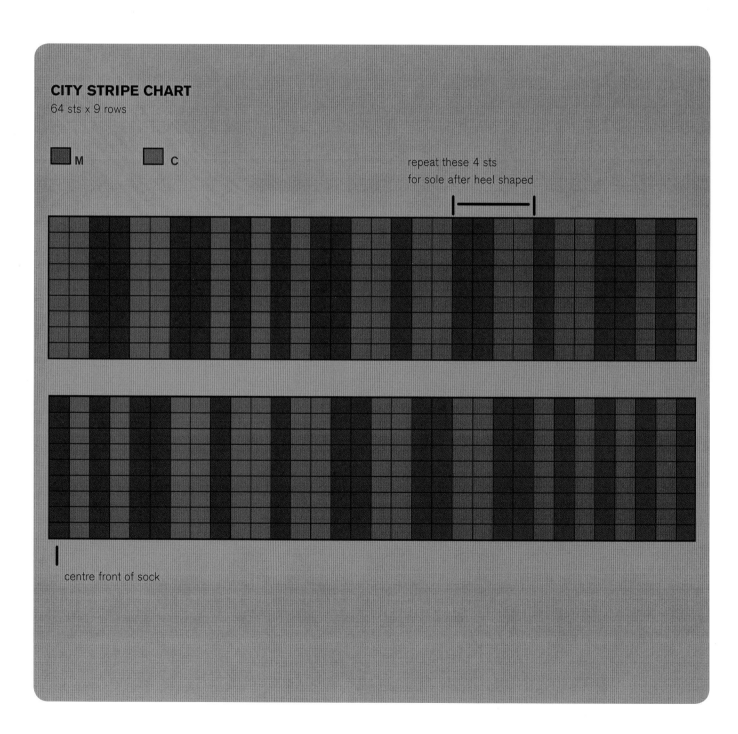

CITY STRIPE CHART
64 sts x 9 rows

M

C

repeat these 4 sts
for sole after heel shaped

centre front of sock

Stepping out

These easy-to-make, innovative socks are worked sideways using circular needles. Add some pretty buttons for a fun way to fasten the flaps.

SIZE
- To suit: small (medium, large) women's sizes

TENSION
- 30 sts and 40 rows to 4in (10cm) in st st using 3.25mm needles
- Use larger or smaller needles to achieve correct tension

MATERIALS AND EQUIPMENT
- Colinette Jitterbug 100% Merino Wool (267m per 100g)
- 2 x 100g hanks Fruit Coulis
- Pair of 3.25mm (UK10:US3) needles
- 2 x 3.25mm (UK10:US3) circular needles
- 6 buttons

SPECIAL TECHNIQUES
- Use of circular needles
- Raised increase
- Heel stitch
- Kitchener stitch
- M1L and M1R – see abbreviations (see page 48)

NOTE
The socks are worked back and forth using a circular needle, which provides the flexibility to take the curve of the heel and toe. A second circular needle is used for grafting.

LEG AND FOOT
Using a provisional cast-on method, cast on 97 (98, 99) sts. On the first row, markers are placed to divide the sections of the sock, and on the second row the stitch patterns used for each section are established.

Row 1: (WS) p38 (38, 37) foot sts, place foot marker; p13 (14, 15) heel sts, place centre heel marker; p13 (13, 14) heel sts, place leg marker; k8 (8, 8) leg sts, place cuff marker; p25 cuff sts.

Row 2: (RS) work the 25 cuff sts in d-g st (see below; beg with row 1), work the leg and heel sts and up to the last foot sts in st st; work the edge stitch in the slip stitch edge patt (see below; beg with row 1). Work in the stitch patts as set for 5 further rows.

DOUBLE GARTER STITCH
Row 1: (RS) Purl.
Row 2: (WS) Knit.
Row 3: (RS) Knit.
Row 4: (WS) Purl.

SLIP STITCH EDGE
Row 1: (RS) Sl 1 st p-wise with yarn in front.
Row 2: (WS) K1 tbl.

SHAPE HEEL
Row 8: Cont in the stitch patts as set, and at the same time, begin the heel shaping by working paired dec every row thus:
RS rows: Work to 2 sts before the centre heel marker, k2tog, skpo, k to end.
WS rows: Work to 2 sts before centre heel marker, ssp, p2tog, work to end.

Rep appropriate dec rows 11 (12, 13) times. Keep the centre heel and cuff markers, and add a centre toe marker 2 sts in from end of the foot (the slip st edge st counts as one of these sts).

SHAPE TOE

Row 20 (21, 21): Begin working paired inc every row thus:

RS rows: Work to 1 st before the centre toe marker, M1R, k2, M1L, work to end.

WS rows: Work to 1 st before the centre toe marker, M1L, p2, M1R, work to end.

Rep the inc row until there are 13 (15, 16) sts between the centre toe marker and the end of the toe, which should be row 31 (33, 35).

Work 16 rows without increasing.

Row 48 (50, 52): Begin working paired dec on every row thus:

RS rows: Work to 2 sts before the centre toe marker, k2tog, skpo, work to end.

WS rows: Work to 2 sts before centre toe marker, ssp, p2tog, work to end.

Rep the dec row 11 (12, 13) more times.

SHAPE HEEL

Row 60 (63, 66): Begin second half of heel shaping by working paired inc every row thus:

RS rows: Work to 1 st before centre heel marker, M1R, k2, M1L, work to end.

WS rows: Work to 1 st before centre heel marker, M1L, p2, M1R, and work to end.

Rep the inc row 11 (12,13) more times.

Work straight ending with row 79 (83, 91).

SHAPE CUFF OVERLAP

Work 16 rows on cuff sts only.

Cast off 16 cuff sts at either side.

MAKING UP

Remove the provisional cast on and place the resulting 'live' loops on the second circular needle.

Cut the working yarn, leaving a long tail, and thread this on a tapestry needle.

Fold sock in half, RS together, and place needles parallel to one another.

Holding the needles in your left hand and working right to left, graft the two sides together using Kitchener stitch.

Fold flap over and attach buttons through both flap pieces at the back of the heel.

Pair and a spare

No need to worry about lost socks with this design
– just work three in co-ordinating shades.
They are great fun and ideal for children.

SIZE
- To fit ankle circumference 8in (20cm)
- Heel to toe 7in (18cm)

TENSION
- 30 sts and 42 rows to 4in (10cm) on 2.5mm needles

MATERIALS AND EQUIPMENT
- Cygnet 4-ply 75% wool, 25% nylon (205m per 50g)
- 2 x 50g balls red (M)
- Regia multi sock yarn 75% wool, 25% polyamide (210m per 50g ball)
- 2 x 50g balls orange/blue/yellow (C)
- Set of 2.5mm (UK13:US1) double-pointed needles

SPECIAL TECHNIQUES
- Kitchener stitch
- Easy heel

BASIC SOCK

Cast on 64 sts divided so there are 32 sts on N1, 16 sts on N2 and 16 sts on N3. Using M, work 15 rounds k1, p1 rib.

Next round: * K4, yo, k2 tog, rep from * to end for eyelets.

Change to C and work 4 rounds st st. Check that there are 32 sts on N1 for top of foot; 16 on N2 and 16 on N3.

Note: The sts on N2 and N3 form the heel; inc points are where N2 and N3 meet either end of N1.

EASY HEEL

Inc round: K sts on N1; inc 1, k sts on N2, k to last st on N3, inc 1.

Next and every alternate round: K all sts. Rep until there are 32 sts on N1, 30 sts on N2 and 30 sts on N3.

Decrease round: K across 32 sts on N1, then k2tog, k1 from N2 on to N1, turn.

Next row: Sl1, p to end, then p2tog, p1 using 3 sts from next needle, turn.

Next row: Sl1, k to end of needle; from next needle k2tog, k1, turn.

Next row: Sl1, k to end of needle; from next needle k2tog, k1 turn.

Next row: Sl1, p to end; from next needle p2 tog, p1.

Work as set until there are 16 sts on N1, 30 sts on N2 and 30 sts on N3.

FOOT

Work 35 rounds C.

TOE

Round 1: Using M, k to 2 sts from end of N1, sl2 k-wise, k1 from N2 and pass slipped sts over; work across N2 to last 2 sts, sl2 k-wise, k1 from N3 and pass slipped sts over.

Round 2 K all sts.

Rep last 2 rounds until 12 sts rem across all needles.

VARIATION 1

Using C, cast on 64 sts and work 13 rounds k1, p1 rib.

Change to M and work 2 rounds k.

Next round: * K4, yo, k2 tog, rep from * to end for eyelets.

Next round: K all sts using M.

Next round: Change to C and k all sts.

Work 3 rows C.

HEEL INCREASES

Work as for basic sock.

Knit 35 rounds C.

Change to M for toe.

TOE

Round 1: K to 2 sts from end of N1, sl2 k-wise, k1 from N2 and psso the k1, work across N2 to last 2 sts, sl2 k-wise, k1 from N3 and psso the k1.

Round 2: K all sts.

Rep last 2 rounds until 12 sts rem across all needles.

VARIATION 2

Using C, work 15 rounds k1, p1 rib.

Next round: * K4, yo, k2 tog, rep from * to end for eyelets.

Work 1 round C, 7 rounds M, 4 rounds C, 3 rounds M, 7 rounds C.

Next round: *K2M, k2C, rep from * to end.

HEEL INCREASES

Work as for basic sock using M.

FOOT

Work 3 rounds C, 2 rounds M and 3 rounds C.

Next round: *K2C, k2M, rep from * to end.

Rep last round twice more.

Next round: *K2M, k2C, rep from * to end.

Rep last round twice more.

Work 4 rounds C in g-st.

Work 3 rounds M.

Next round *K2M, k2C, rep from * to end.

Rep last round 3 times more.

Work 3 rounds C, 10 rounds M, 1 round C.

TOE

Shape as for basic sock using C.

MAKING UP

Cut the yarn and graft sts tog using Kitchener stitch.

Sole mates

Fabulous for wearing around the house, these look just like shoes and socks! If you do not fancy the bow, instructions are given for an alternative frilled trim.

SIZE
- Ankle circumference 8in (20.5cm)
- Toe to heel 9in (23cm)

TENSION
- 24 sts and 28 rows to 4in (10cm) over stocking stitch using 3.25mm needles
- Use larger or smaller needles to achieve correct tension

MATERIALS AND EQUIPMENT
- Araucania Ranco 75% wool, 25% nylon (376yd per 100g skein)
- 1 x 100g skein 483 (M)
- 1 x 100g skein multi 502 (C)
- Set of 3.25mm (UK10:US3) double-pointed needles

SPECIAL TECHNIQUES
- Wrapped stitches (see Techniques, page 47)
- The sock is worked from the toe up

TOE
Cast on 8 sts and work 6 rows st st to form a rectangle.

Turn so that WS of work is facing.

Round 1: Using N1, k8 along working edge of rectangle; using N2 pick up and k6 from next side; using N3 pick up and k8 from next side; using N4 pick up and k6 from final edge. Work in g-st thus:

Round 2: K8, m1 on N1; k6, m1 on N2; k8, m1 on N3; k6, m1 on N4 (32 sts).

Round 3: K9, m1 on N1; k7 on N2; k9, m1 on N3; k7 on N4 (34 sts).

Round 4: K10, m1 on N1; k7, m1 on N2; k10, m1 on N3; k7, m1 on N4 (38 sts).

Round 5: K11, m1 on N1; k8 on N2; k11, m1 on N3; k8 on N4 (40 sts).

Round 6: K12, m1 on N1; k8, m1 on N2; k12, m1 on N3; k8, m1 on N4 (44 sts).

Round 7: K13, m1 on N1; k9, m1 on N2; k13, m1 on N3; k9, m1 on N4 (48 sts).

Round 8: K14, m1 on N1; k10 on N2; k14, m1 on N3; k10 on N4 (50 sts).

Round 9: K15, m1 on N1; k10 on N2; k15, m1 on N3; k10 on N4 (52 sts).

Round 10: K16, m1 on N1; k10, m1 on N2; k16, m1 on N3; k10, m1 on N4 (56 sts).

Round 11: K17, m1 on N1 ; k11, m1 on N2; k17, m1 on N3; k11, m1 on N4 (60 sts).

Round 12: K18 on N1; k12 on N2; k18 on N3; k12 on N4 (60 sts).

FOOT
Next round: On N1 g-st in M; on N2 g-st in M; on N3 st st in C; on N4 g-st in M. Cont in this way for 50 rows (or to length required).

HEEL

With RS facing and using C, begin short row shaping using sts on N1, N2 and N4 (42 sts)

Row 1: K19, wrap 1, turn.

Row 2: P19 wrap 1, turn.

Rep rows 1 and 2 until 14 sts remain.

Next row: K14, pick up and k wrapped st, replace on L needle, turn.

Next row: P14, pick up and p wrapped st, replace on L needle, turn.

Next row: K15, pick up and k wrapped st, replace on L needle, turn.

Next row: P15, pick up and p wrapped st, replace on L needle, turn.

Rep these rows until all stitches are back on the needles.

Divide sts between three needles and resume working in the round.

Work 38 rounds (or length required).

Work 8 further rounds for a sock with a bow OR work alternative frilled top (see right).

BOW

Cast on 18 sts and k 14 rows.

Cast off.

ALTERNATIVE FRILLED TOP
(no bow)

Next round: K all 60 sts

Next round: *K1, m1, rep from * to end. (120 sts).

Work 3 rounds st st.

Next round: *K1 m1, rep from* to end. (240 sts).

Work 2 rounds st st.

Cast off.

MAKING UP

Fold bow piece ends to middle.

Place seam downwards and attach to front of sock to form a bow.

Darn in ends.

Snug slouch

This young, fun design is just right for relaxing at home. The yarn is used double throughout for extra snugness.

SIZE
- To suit UK size 4–5 (5–6, 6–7)
- Foot length 8½ (9½, 10½)in/22 (24, 27)cm

TENSION
- 11 sts and 15 rows to 4in (10cm) over patt on 7mm needles, using yarn double throughout
- Use larger or smaller needles to achieve correct tension

MATERIALS AND EQUIPMENT
- Cygnet Aran, 75% British wool and 25% polyamide (224m per 100g).
- 3 x 100g balls 233 Lavender
- Set of 7mm (UK2:US10.5) double-pointed needles

SPECIAL TECHNIQUES
- M1
- Kitchener stitch

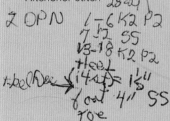

LEG
Cast on 28 (30, 32) sts divided evenly between 4 needles.
Join, taking care not to twist sts.

Size 4–5 only: K1, *p2, k2 rep from * to last 3 sts, p2, k1. Rep until work measures 10in (26cm).

Size 5–6 only: K1, p3 *p2, k2, rep from * to last 4 sts, p3, k1.
Rep until sock measures 5in (12cm), then dec 1 st in each p3 section (28 sts).
Next round: K1, p2 *p2, k2, rep from * to last 4 sts, p2, k1.
Cont until work measures 10½in (26cm).

Size 6–7 only: K1, p4, *p2, k2, rep from * to last 7 sts, k2, p4, k1. Rep until sock measures 5½in (14cm), then dec 1 st in each p4 section (30 sts).
Next round: K1, p3 *p2, k2, rep from * to last 4 sts, p3, k1. Cont until work measures 11in (28cm), then dec 1 st in each p3 section.
Next round: K1, p3 *p2, k2, rep from * to last 4 sts, p3, k1.
Cont until work measures 12in (30cm).

DIVIDE FOR HEEL
(all sizes)
Set aside 14 sts (7 sts on either side) for gusset and work back on the rem 14 sts for heel for 2 (2½, 3)in or 5 (6, 7)cm. Place marking thread here.

DECREASE FOR HEEL
Row 1: K until 5 (6, 6)sts left on row, k2tog turn.
Row 2: P until 5 (6, 7)sts left on row, p2tog turn.
Row 3: K until 4 (5, 5)sts left on row, k2tog, turn.

Row 4: P until 4 (5, 5) sts left on row, p2tog turn.

Cont in this way, leaving one st fewer before each dec, until 6 (7, 8) sts rem.

FOOT

Pick up 7 (9, 10) sts on each side of heel. Arrange all 34 (38, 42) sts, including those set aside, on double-pointed needles.

Next round: Work the centre 16 sts in rib and the rest in st st.

Next round: Work in st st and rib but dec by working k2tog into the back of the 2 sts before the rib and working the 2 sts after the rib as k2 tog.

Rep last 2 rounds until 24 (26, 28) sts rem. Work straight until foot measures approx 7 (8, 8½)in or 18 (20, 22)cm from heel.

Insert a marker thread on each side 12 (13, 14) sts between each marker.

DECREASE FOR TOE

Cont in st st on all sts, dec on either side of each marker thread (MT) thus:

Next round: K2tog, k1, MT, k1, k2tog into back of st.

Next round: Work in st st.

Rep the last 2 rows a total of 3 times

Dec on every row 1 (1, 2) times (8, 10, 8) sts.

MAKING UP

Using Kitchener stitch graft sts together.

Boot sock

If your man needs some colourful persuasion to venture into the great outdoors, these may do the trick! They are guaranteed to keep out the cold.

SIZE
- To suit ankle circumference 8–13in (20–33cm)
- Toe to heel 11½ in (29cm) adjustable

TENSION
Not critical, as fabric is stretchy.

MATERIALS AND EQUIPMENT
- Cygnet Wool-rich Machine-washable Chunky (148m per 100g)
- 1 x 100g ball in 2148 Petrole (A)
- 1 x 100g ball in 0268 Olive (B)
- 1 x 100g ball in 2185 Geranium (C)
- Set of 4mm (UK6:US8) double-pointed needles

SPECIAL TECHNIQUES
- W1 = wrap 1
- Short row shaping
- Kitchener stitch

METHOD
Cast on 48 sts divided evenly between four needles.
Join, taking care not to twist sts.
Place marker at beg of round between N1 and N4.
Work in k2, p2 rib and in stripe pattern:

STRIPE PATTERN
*8 rows A,
8 rows B,
1 row A, 8 rows C,
8 rows A,
5 rows B,
1 row A,
8 rows C,
7 rows B,
8 rows C,
8 rows A,

1 row C,
8 rows B,
rep from *as desired, working a single row of B between C and A on the foot.
Work striped rib for 18in (46cm) or desired length.

SHAPE HEEL
Use 20 sts, RS facing.
Row 1: K19, W1.
Row 2: P19 W1.
Rep last 2 rows working one stitch fewer (i.e. 18 sts on next 2 rows; 17 sts for following 2 rows) until 11 sts rem in work.
Next row: K11, pick up and k wrapped st, replace on LH needles, turn.
Next row: P11, pick up and p wrapped st, replace on LH needles, turn.
Next row: K12, pick up and k wrapped st,

replace on LH needles, turn.

Next row: P12, pick up and p wrapped st, replace on LH needles, turn. Cont as set working one more st on each row until all 20 heel sts are back in work, then cont in rib patt across rest of sock (48 sts). Work straight in st st (heel sts) and rib (upper sock) following stripe patt until sock 2in (5cm) shorter than required for toe.

SHAPE TOE

Note: the toe is worked in a two-colour vertical stripe of 1 st A, 1 st B and the 2 st stripe sequence kept correct throughout.

Divide sts equally between four needles (12 sts per needle) and shape thus:

DECREASE ROUND

N1: K to last 3 sts, k2tog, k1.
N2: K1, skpo, k to end.
N3: K to last 3 sts, k2tog, k1.
N4: K1, skpo, k to end.
Cont as set, alternating dec and non-dec rounds, until 32 sts rem.
Work each round as a dec round until 8 sts rem.

MAKING UP

Graft 8 sts tog using Kitchener stitch.
Weave in any loose ends of yarn.

Vertical stripes

The yarn used for this design was developed to produce socks with horizontal stripes – but this pattern is worked sideways, so the result is vertical stripes!

SIZE
- To fit size small (medium, large) adult sizes

TENSION
- 30 sts and 40 rows to 4in (10cm) in st st using 3.25mm needles
- Use larger or smaller needles to achieve correct tension

MATERIALS AND EQUIPMENT
- Kaffe Fassett for Regia 75% Wool and 25% Polyamide (210m per 50g)
- 3 x 50g balls 4256 Mirage Twilight
- 2 x 3.25mm (UK10:US3) circular needles

SPECIAL TECHNIQUES
- Kitchener stitch
- Right-slanting dec: k2tog or p2tog
- Left-slanting dec: skpo or ssp
- M1R (see Techniques, page 46)
- M1L (see Techniques, page 46)

NOTE
The socks are worked back and forth on a circular needle, which has the flexibility to accommodate the curve of the heel and toe. All even rows are RS rows, and all odd rows are WS rows. A second circular needle in the same size is used for grafting.

METHOD
Note: markers are placed to divide the sections of the sock on row 1. The patterns used for each section are established on row 2.

Using a provisional cast-on method, cast on 113 (117, 118) sts.

Row 1: (WS) P38 (38, 37) foot sts, place foot marker; p13 (14, 15) heel sts, place centre heel marker; p13 (14, 15) heel sts, place leg marker; k41 (43, 43) leg sts, place cuff marker; p8 cuff sts.

Row 2: Work the cuff sts in dg-st (see right), starting with row 1 of patt; work the leg sts and heel sts in st st; work up to the last foot sts in st st, then work the edge st in the slip-stitch edge patt starting with row 1.

DOUBLE GARTER STITCH
Row 1 (RS): Purl.
Row 2 (WS): Knit.
Row 3 (RS): Knit.
Row 4 (WS): Purl.

SLIP-STITCH EDGE
Row 1 (RS): Sl1 p-wise with yarn in front.
Row 2 (WS): K1 tbl.
Cont in patts as set, work 5 rows.

HEEL SHAPING (1)
Row 8: Cont in patts as set, begin heel shaping by working paired dec on every row thus:
RS rows: Work to 2 sts before centre heel marker, k2tog, skpo, work to end.
WS rows: Work to 2 sts before centre heel marker, ssp, p2tog, work to end.
Rep this row 11 (12,13) times.

CALF SHAPING

Row 19 (20, 21): Work as a dec row,.
At the same time reposition the stitch
markers, retaining the centre heel and cuff
markers, removing the leg and the foot
markers, and adding a centre toe marker
2 sts in from the end of the foot (inc
edge st).
After this row, there should be 8 cuff sts,
41 (43, 43) edge sts, 2 heel sts and 38
(38, 37) foot sts or 89 (91, 90) sts.

TOE SHAPING

Row 20 (21, 22): Begin to work paired inc
on every row thus:
RS rows: Work to 1 st before centre toe
marker, M1R, k2, M1L, work to end.
WS rows: Work to 1 st before centre toe
marker, M1L, p2, M1R, work to end.
Rep inc row 11 (12, 13) times until there
are 13 (15, 16) sts between the centre toe
marker and the end of the toe.
Row 31 (33, 35): This completes the toe
increases. After this row, there should be 8
cuff sts, 42 (44, 47) sts between the cuff
and centre heel markers, 49 (50, 50) sts
between the centre heel and centre toe
markers, and 14 (15, 16) sts from the
centre toe marker to the end of the row, a
total of 113 (117, 118) sts.
Work 8 rows.

COMPLETE TOE

Row 48 (50, 52): Begin working paired
dec on every row thus:
RS rows: Work to 2 sts before centre toe
marker, k2tog, skpo, work to end.
WS rows: Work to 2 sts before centre toe
marker, ssp, p2tog, work to end. Rep dec
row 11 (12, 13) times so there are 8 cuff
sts, 41 (43, 43) leg sts, 2 heel sts (1 st
either side of centre heel marker) and 38
(38, 37) foot sts, 89 (91, 90) sts in total.

HEEL SHAPING (2)

Row 60 (63, 66): Begin working paired
inc for second half of heel shaping on
every row thus:
RS rows: Work to 1 st before centre heel
marker, M1R, k2, M1L, work to end.
WS rows: Work to 1 st before centre heel
marker, M1L, p2, M1R, work to end.
Rep inc row 11 (12, 13) times and at the
same time:
Row 68 (72, 76): Cont to work the leg sts
in g st.
Row 71 (75, 79): This should be the last
row of heel increases. After this, there
should be 8 cuff sts, 54 (57, 58) sts
between the cuff and centre heel markers,
51 (52, 52) sts between the centre heel
marker and end of row, 113 (117, 118) sts.
Work straight for a further 8 rows ending
with row 79 (83, 91).

MAKING UP

Remove the provisional cast on and place
the resulting 'live' loops on the second
circular needle.
Cut the working yarn leaving a long tail, and
thread this on a tapestry needle.
Fold work in half, RS together, bring
needles parallel to one another and,
working from right to left, graft the two
sides together.
Working along the sides of the foot and
toe, pick up the sts between the edge sts
so you have 20 (21, 22) sts on the needle.
Graft these sts together in the same way
as the main sock seam.
Turn finished sock inside out to produce
the effect.

Whizzy walkers

These should be snazzy enough to make your man go that extra mile in his walking boots. They have an interesting squared heel, and the pattern is based on old tiles.

SIZE
- Ankle circumference 8in (20cm)
- Toe to heel 9in (22.5cm)

TENSION
- 24 sts and 28 rounds to 4in (10cm) measured over patt.
- Use larger or smaller needles to achieve correct tension

MATERIALS AND EQUIPMENT
- 4-ply sock wool (approx 198yd per 50g ball)
- 2 x 50g balls brown (M)
- 2 x 50g balls cream (C)
- Set of 4mm (UK8:US6) double-pointed needles

SPECIAL TECHNIQUES
- Double decrease: slip 2 sts, k1, pass both sl sts over k st

NOTE
The examples have been worked using the same yarn, but with the main and contrast reversed for the second sock.

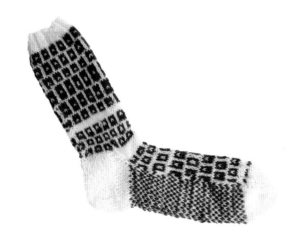

LEG
Using M, cast on 50 sts and divide evenly between 3 needles. Join into a round being careful not to twist sts.

Note: this join marks a seam and the beginning of a round, so place a marker here if desired.

Work 6 rows k1, p1 rib.

Next round: Inc 1 st at each end of round (52 sts).

Beg working pattern from chart to marked row, but dec 1 st at each end on last round (50 sts).

Divide sts so there are 12 sts on N1, 25 sts on N2 and 13 sts on N3 (seam line between N1 and N3).

Using N3, k across 11 sts on N1; yf, sl1. Set aside the 25 sts on N2 for instep and work the heel on 25 sts.

Turn work.

SHAPE HEEL
Row 1: K1 tbl, p23, yf, sl1, turn.

Row 2: K1tbl, *k1, sl1 p-wise, rep from * to end, turn.

Row 3: K16, k2tog tbl, turn.

Row 4: *Sl1, p7, p2tog, turn.

Row 5: Sl1 (K1, sl1) three times, k1, k2tog tbl, turn.

Rep last 2 rows until all sts either side of 9 central heel sts have been worked off.

GUSSET
Next row: Using N1 (Sl1, k1) 4 times, k1, pick up 13 sts tbl along R heel flaps; using N2, pick up and k1 st tbl at beg of instep sts, k across 25 instep sts; pick up and k1 st at end of instep; using N3, k13 tbl from L of heel flap, slip the first 4 sts from heel flap on to N3. There should now be 18 sts on N1, 27 sts on N2 and 17 sts on N3.

Next round: K to last 2 sts on N1, k2tog;

work k2tog tbl at the beg of N2, k to last 2 sts, k2 tog; at the beg of N3 k2tog tbl, k to end.

Next round: Follow patt on top of foot and at the same time dec 1 st at the end of N1 and the beg of N3 as before.

Repeat until there are 13 sts on N1, 25 sts on N2 and 12 sts on N3

Work straight, working chart B twice on top of foot and sole in M until foot measures 2.5cm less than length required.

Cont in M only.

SHAPE TOE

Round 1: K to last 2 sts on N1, sl2 k-wise; k1 from N2 and pass slipped sts from N1 over this k1, work to last 2 sts on N2, sl2 k-wise; k1 from N3 and pass slipped sts from N2 over this K1.

Round 2: K.

Rep last 2 rows until 6 sts rem on N1, 13 sts on N2, 6 sts on N3.

Now work double dec every round until 6 sts in total rem.

MAKING UP

Draw thread through rem sts and draw up. Weave loose end firmly back into work and stitch to finish.

ANKLE AND TOP OF FOOT CHART

12 sts x 38 rows

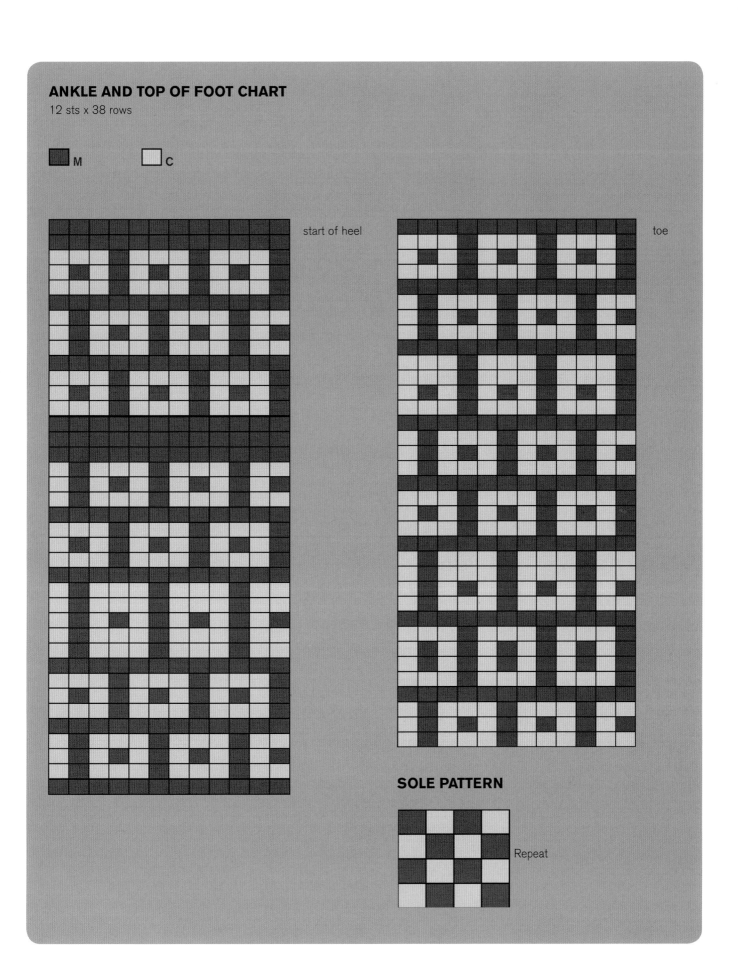

■ M   □ C

start of heel

toe

SOLE PATTERN

Repeat

Techniques

Knitting socks is fun and surprisingly easy, but taking the time to read through these guidelines before you begin will greatly increase your chance of success. Socks are usually worked in rounds, rather than rows, on circular or double-pointed needles. The advantage of this is that there are no seams to sew up, or to rub!

The foot section of a good basic sock should be roughly one-third the length of the finished sock. Check the actual measurements of the foot and leg before you begin, and adjust the pattern if necessary. Experiment with different heel and toe styles, then incorporate your favourites in any design you make.

HOW TO KNIT A SOCK

Cast on firmly, but cast off fairly loosely. For extra elasticity, cast on twice as many stitches as required for the top of the sock, then work two stitches together all the way along the first row to return to the correct number. Work as evenly as possible to prevent your socks from losing their shape in the wash.

For a knee-high sock, work the ribbing, then work approximately as many rounds are there stitches on the needles before starting to decrease. Work decreases on each side of the central 'seam' stitch, until at the ankle the number of stitches is approximately three-quarters of the number cast on.

For the ankle section, work approximately as many rounds are there are stitches on the needle before starting to decrease. Then, keeping the 'seam' stitch central, place half the stitches on a needle for the heel. Divide the remaining stitches equally between two needles for the instep, and set aside until the heel has been worked.

The length of the finished heel, laid flat, should be the same as the width of the ankle. Pick up as many stitches along the heel flap as are on the needle at the top of the heel and the instep – roughly 8–10 fewer stitches than the number of stitches cast on. If there are fewer loops than stitches that need to be picked up, increase evenly as necessary.

For the gusset, decrease on alternate rounds until there are the same number of stitches as on the ankle. The toe of an average-sized adult sock should be about 2½in (5cm) long.

TENSION

When you begin to knit socks, start a habit that will save a lot of time in the end: work a swatch using the chosen yarn and needles. These can be labelled and filed for future reference. Many sock yarns are a 4-ply weight. When knitting socks in 4-ply,

> ### TIP
> Work a swatch of yarn until you are happy with the effect. Measure carefully to calculate the number of stitches you need. Deduct approximately 10 per cent to allow for the sock to stretch and ensure a snug fit. Make sure the resulting number is divisible by four.

a tension of 68 sts to 4in (10cm) width on size 2.25mm (UK13–14/US0–1) needles or 48 sts on size 3.5mm (UK9–10/US4) works well.

Needles

Most of the socks in this book are worked on double-pointed needles. For sections of the sock that are not worked in the round, such as heels and gussets, use the same needles and work back and forth. Socks may also be worked using circular needles if preferred. A few designs are worked on straight needles, so there are seams to join. Others are worked back and forth on circular needles.

Yarn

Socks may be made in a huge variety of yarns, from luxurious cashmere to smooth, cool cotton. There are also many yarns on the market that are specifically designed for socks. A good choice for socks is a yarn made mainly from wool for warmth, with a little added nylon for strength.

Substituting yarn

It is relatively easy to substitute different yarns for any of the socks in this book, but do check the tension. One way to substitute yarn is to work out how many wraps per inch (wpi) the yarn produces. Do this by winding it closely, in a single layer, around a rule or similar object and counting how many 'wraps' to an inch (2.5cm) it produces. For a successful result, pick a yarn that produces twice, or a little more than twice, the number of wraps per inch as there are stitches per inch in the tension swatch.

Tension required	Number of wraps per inch produced by yarn
8 sts per in (4-ply/ fingering)	16–18 wpi
6.5 sts per in (DK/sport)	13–14 wpi
5.5 sts per in (chunky/ worsted)	11–12 wpi

Measurements

For a standard sock, the width of the leg is the same as the width of the foot. For a good fit, measure the widest part of the leg and the widest part of the foot. One way to achieve a perfect fit is to work the sock from the toe up, which also eliminates the need to graft stitches on the toe. Another method is to work socks as a tube, leaving aside the heel area, which is worked last. This method is ideal when following a complicated charted design.

> ***TIP***
>
> Quick converter – use our quick guide to find your size
>
> Adult female
> 8 –10½in (20–26.5cm)
>
> Adult male
> 10½–12in (27–30.5cm)

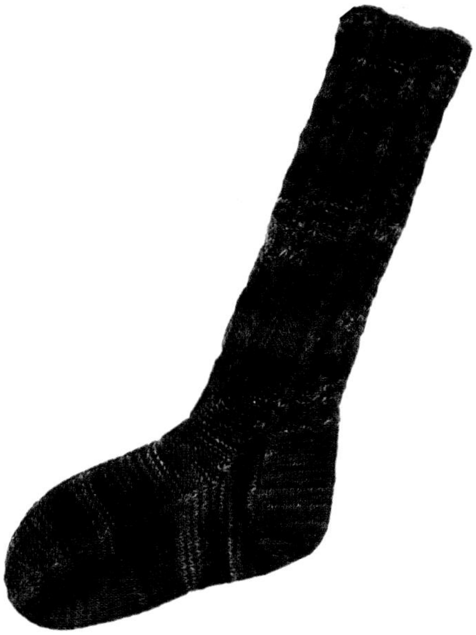

SIZE CHARTS

Babies & Toddlers

Size/age of baby	Foot length
3–5lb	2½in–3in (6–7.5cm)
5–7lb	3–3½in (7.5–9cm)
7–9lb (most common size for newborns)	3½–3¾in (8.25–9.5cm)
3–6 months	4–4½in (10–11.5cm)
6 months–1 year	4¼–4¾in (10.5–12cm)
18 months–2 years	5–5½in (12.5–14cm)

Children & Adults

European shoe size	UK shoe size	US shoe size	Width round top of cuff	Heel flap length	Total foot length
Infants/toddlers					
18-20	1½–4	2½–5	5⅓in (13.5cm)	1in (2.5cm)	5⅛in (13cm)
22-23	5–6½	6–7½	5⅞in (15cm)	1⅛in (2.75cm)	5⅞in (15cm)
24-25	7–7½	8–8½	6⅛in (15.5cm)	1⅓in (3.5cm)	6in (16cm)
Children					
26-27	8-9	8½–9½	6⅜in (16cm)	1½in (4cm)	7⅛in (18cm)
28-29	10–11	10½–11½	6⅔in (16.75cm)	1½in (4cm)	7in (19cm)
30-31	11½–12½	12–13	6⅞in (17.5cm)	1¾in (4.5cm)	8⅛in (20.5cm)
Children/adult women					
32-33	13–1	13½–1½	7¼in (18.5cm)	1¾in (4.5cm)	8⅔ in (22cm)
34-35	2–2½	4½–5	7½in (19cm)	1⅞in (4.75cm)	9⅛in (23cm)
36-37	3–4	6–6½	7¾in (19.5cm)	1⅞in (4.75cm)	9⅝in (24.5cm)
38-39	5–6	7½–8½	8in (20.25cm)	2⅛in (5.25cm)	10¼in (26cm)
40-41	7–7½	9½–10	8¼in (20.5cm)	2¼in (5.5cm)	10⅝in (27cm)
42-43	8–9	10½–11	8½in (21.5cm)	2¼in (5.75in)	11in (28cm)
Adult men					
42-43	8-9	9–10	8½in (21.5cm)	2¼in (2.75cm)	11in (28cm)
44-45	10–10½	11–11½	9in (22.75cm)	2½in (6.5cm)	11½in (29cm)
46-47	11–12	12–13	9⅛in (23cm)	2½in (6.5cm)	12in (30.5cm)

Casting on

There are several well-known ways to cast on. Everyone has a favourite, but it is essential that the cast-on should be elastic. Here are three:

BASIC CAST ON
This method produces a purl stitch as a base.

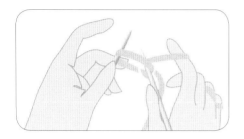  

1 Make a slip knot and place on the left-hand needle. Insert the right-hand needle into the loop and wrap the yarn around the needles as shown.

2 Using the point of the right-hand needle, pull the yarn through the first loop to create a second loop.

3 Slide the loop on to the left-hand needle so there are two loops on the needle. Repeat steps 2 and 3 until the desired number of stitches are on the needle.

CONTINENTAL OR LONG TAIL CAST ON

This makes a firm, smoothly twisted elastic edge, using only one needle.

- Make a slip knot and place on the tip of the right-hand needle. Leave a tail about three times as long as the edge you want to cast on. Take the tail behind your left thumb and the working yarn around your forefinger, and secure the long ends using your remaining fingers. Twist your wrist so your palm is upwards, then spread your thumb and index finger so the yarn forms a V-shape.

- Slide the needle through the loop on your thumb and catch the working yarn around your forefinger from right to left. Draw the new stitch through, letting the loop slip off your thumb and over the tip of the needle. Catch the tail of the yarn again and pull gently to tighten the new stitch.

- Repeat until required number of stitches are on needle.

TIP
Whichever method you choose, it is vital to check the elasticity of the cast-on. Remember that the sock needs enough stretch to go over the foot then be pulled up and stay up! If you tend to cast on tightly, use a needle one size larger for the cast on.

PROVISIONAL CAST ON

Using this method, you will be able to work in either direction from the starting point

- Make a loop near the end of the working yarn and pull up tight on needle. Take some waste yarn the length of the cast on you need plus 15in (40cm) and make a loop near the end. With the needle in your right hand and facing left, slide the loop of waste yarn on to the needle, next

to the loop of working yarn. Hold the tails of both lengths of yarn to keep them out of the way.

- Insert index finger from behind between working and waste yarns. Twist finger 90° clockwise. Slide thumb next to index finger between waste/working yarns and spread yarns apart: index finger should hold waste and thumb working yarn.

Hold the tails of both yarns with the rest of the fingers on your right hand to keep them taut. Twist yarns 90° clockwise and wrap waste yarn around needle.

- Twist yarns 180° clockwise and wrap waste yarn around needle. Twist yarns anti-clockwise 180° and wrap waste yarn around needle. Repeat until desired number of stitches are on the needle.

> **NOTE:**
> When you begin knitting, make sure waste yarn is under the first stitch to hold the loop. Leave in place until you need to use the stitches it is holding.

Casting off

- Knit two stitches using the right-hand needle, then slip the first stitch over the second and let it drop off the needle.

- Knit another stitch so there are two stitches on the right-hand needle. Repeat the process. When only one stitch remains on the left-hand needle, break yarn and thread through the stitch.

THREE-NEEDLE CAST OFF
Divide stitches evenly between two needles and place needles parallel to each other.
Step 1: *Using a third needle, pick up 1 st from N1 and 1 st from N2, and k sts tog. Repeat, so that there are 2 sts on N3.
Step 2: Pass RH st on N3 over LH st on N3 to cast off.
Repeat from * to end.

KNIT STITCH

  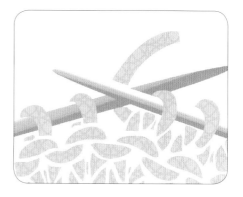

1 Hold the needle with the cast-on stitches in your left hand. Place the tip of the right-hand needle into the first stitch. Wrap the yarn around as for casting on.

2 Pull the yarn through the needle to create a new loop.

3 Slip the new stitch on to the right-hand needle.

Continue in the same way for each stitch on the left-hand needle.

To start a new row, exchange the needles so that the left needle is full once again, then repeat the process.

PURL STITCH

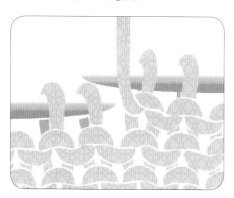 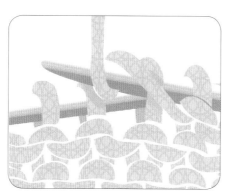 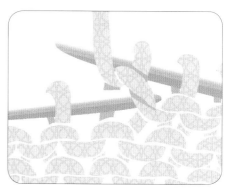

1 Hold the yarn to the front of the work.

2 Place the right needle into the first stitch from front to back. Wrap the yarn around right needle in an anti-clockwise direction.

3 Bring the needle down and back through the stitch, and pull through.

Types of stitches

1   2   3   4   5

1 GARTER STITCH

Knit every row.
In the round, knit 1 row, purl 1 row.

2 STOCKING STITCH

Knit RS rows; purl WS rows.
In the round, knit every row.

3 SINGLE RIB

With an even number of stitches:
Row 1: *k1, p1* rep to end.
Rep for each row.
With an odd number of stitches:
Row 1: *k1, p1, rep from * to last stitch, k1.
Row 2: *p1, k1, rep from * to last stitch, p1

4 DOUBLE RIB

Row 1: *k2, p2, rep from * to end.
Rep for each row.

5 MOSS STITCH

Starting with an even number of stitches:
Row 1: (K1, P1) to end.
Row 2: (P1, K1) to end.
Rep rows 1 and 2 to form pattern.
Starting with an odd number of stitches:
Row 1: *K1, P1, rep from * to last st, K1.
Rep to form pattern.

CABLE STITCH

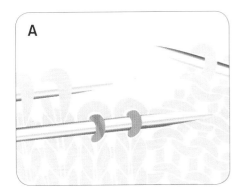

A

B

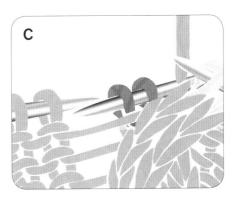

C

These decorative stitches are easy to work using a cable needle. Stitches are held on the cable needle, then worked later to create twists. The example shows 2 sts being cabled, but the method is the same for any number of stitches.

Cable 2F
A Slip the next 2 sts on to a cable needle and hold in front of work.
B Knit the next 2 sts from the left needle, then k2 from the cable needle.

Cable 2B
C Slip 2 sts on to a cable needle and hold at back of work; k2 from left needle, then k2 from cable needle.

Working in the round

Many knitters are scared to try working in the round, but it is quite easy once you have mastered the basics. It is also the fastest way to knit: there are no seams to join, and the right side of the work is always facing, so working patterns is easier. Here are three ways of knitting in the round:

WORKING WITH DOUBLE-POINTED NEEDLES

These usually come in sets of four or five. Reserve one needle to work with and space the cast-on stitches evenly between the remaining needles

> **TIP**
>
> To avoid the dreaded dpn 'ladder' effect, rearrange the stitches on the needles every few rounds to move the stress points. One way to do this is by working two extra stitches from the next needle. Take care to mark the beginning of the actual round, otherwise you will find it hard to tell where technically it begins.

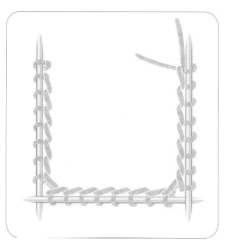

1 Cast on the required number of stitches, divided equally between three needles. Lay the work flat to check that it is not twisted.

2 Insert a fourth needle (the 'working' needle) into the first stitch on needle 3 (N3), and knit the stitch. The yarn will be coming from the last stitch on N1, so working the first stitch will join the work. Pull the first few stitches tighter than in normal knitting to keep the join snug and avoid gaps between stitches. Then simply work the stitches from each needle as you come to it, around and around.

WORKING WITH CIRCULAR NEEDLES

First, choose the correct needle. Its length should be roughly equal to, or less than, the circumference of what you are making. A 16in (40cm) circular needle is ideal for small items, including baby garments and hats. For larger garments, use a 24in (60cm) needle and for a man's sweater use a 29in (75cm) or 32in (80cm) needle. For socks, use the smallest needle available.

Cast on across the right-hand needle so the first stitch is at the tip of the left-hand needle. Before joining the work, place a marker on the right-hand needle. Make sure the ridges at the bottom of the cast-on edge are facing the same way and are not twisted around the needle.

Insert the right-hand needle into the first stitch on the left needle and knit it. Continue to work the stitches from the left-hand to the right-hand needle, pulling the first few stitches firmly to keep the join snug, until you reach the marker. Slip the marker across and continue working around and around, from left to right without turning. The right side of the work will always be facing.

In circular knitting, work stocking stitch by knitting every row. For garter stitch, work one round knit, one round purl.

Magic loop
Magic loop knitting is a technique that allows you to use a circular needle of any

Sock decreases

size. As you work, simply pull the excess loop of cable through at the end of every round. You may prefer this, but try the method described above first.

Working with two circular needles

This idea of working two socks simultaneously on separate circular needles has become increasingly popular. It is appealing because both socks are completed at the same time. To prevent 'ladders', maintain a steady tension, especially near the circular joins.

Choose circular needles 16–24in (40–60cm) long, as appropriate. It is helpful if the needles look different. After casting on, heel stitches remain on needle 1 and instep stitches remain on needle 2.

When stitches are at rest, move them to the flexible section of the needle to provide the necessary 'give'.

- Using the first circular needle, cast on the required number of stitches.
- Slip the instep stitches to a second circular needle.
- Still using the first circular needle, cast on the number of stitches required for the second sock. Take care to cast on to the end of the needle, away from the first sock's yarn supply.
- Slip the instep stitches for the second sock to the second needle. The yarn supply for both socks should now be in the same position.

Methods of decreasing are interchangeable, so choose the one you prefer, but remember to use it consistently for a neat overall appearance. Use a left-slanting decrease at the beginning of a needle and the right-slanting decrease at the end of a needle.

LEFT-SLANTING DECREASES
Ssk
Slip 2 sts knitwise, return sts to left needle, place the needle into the back of the yarn loops and knit them together.

Ssk (variation)
Slip 1st knitwise, then 1 st purlwise. Return the sts to the left needle, then knit them together through the back of loops.

Ssp
Slip 2 sts knitwise, return the sts to the left needle, then purl them together through the back of the loops.

Skpo
Slip 1 st knitwise, k1, then pass the slipped stitch over the knitted st.

K2tog tbl
Knit two stitches together through the back of the yarn loops

RIGHT-SLANTING DECREASE
K2tog
Knit two stitches together through the front of the loops.

Sock increases

There are many different ways to increase stitches, and knitters tend to stick with what they prefer. As with decreases, use the same method of increasing throughout a garment to ensure the best effect.

Simple increase
The easiest way to increase is by working twice into a stitch. To do this knitwise, simply knit the stitch as normal, but do not remove the loop from the left-hand needle. Wrap the yarn over the needle again and knit into the back of the stitch before removing the loop from the left-hand needle.

M1R – make one stitch slanting to the right
Find the horizontal connecting yarn between the needles. Using the left needle, pick up the connecting yarn from the back to the front and leave this 'raised bar' on the left needle. Work the raised bar by knitting (RS row) or purling (WS row) as appropriate.

M1L – make one stitch slanting to the left
Find the horizontal connecting yarn between the needles. Using the left needle, pick up the connecting yarn from the front to the back and leave this 'raised bar' on the left needle. Then either knit the raised bar through the back of the loop (RS row) or purl the raised bar (WS row).

Joining seams

STOCKING STITCH JOINS

The edges of stocking stitch tend to curl so it may be tricky to join. The best way to join is to use mattress stitch to pick up the bars between the columns of stitches.

Working upwards or downwards as preferred, secure yarn to one of the pieces you wish to join. Place the edges of the work together and pick up a bar from one side, then the corresponding bar from the opposite side. Repeat. After a few stitches, pull gently on the yarn and the two sides will come together in a seam that is almost invisible. Take care to stay in the same column all the way. Do not pull the stitches tight at the beginning as you will not be able to see what you are doing.

GARTER STITCH JOINS

It is easier to join garter stitch as it has a firm edge and lies flat. Place the edges of the work together, right side up, and see where the stitches line up. Pick up the bottom loops of stitches on one side of the work and the top loops of the stitches on the other side. After a few stitches, pull gently on the yarn. The stitches should lock together and lie completely flat. The inside of the join should look the same as the outside.

KITCHENER STITCH/ KITCHENER GRAFTING

This is a method of grafting stitches invisibly together.

METHOD

Divide the stitches you wish to join evenly between two double-pointed needles. Hold both needles parallel in your left hand, so that the working yarn is to your right, and is coming off the first stitch on the back needle. Cut the working yarn to a reasonable working length.

- Using a third needle, purl the first stitch on the front needle.
- Drop the stitch off the left front needle, and pull the yarn all the way through the dropped stitch so that there is no longer a stitch on the right (working) needle.
- Knit the next stitch on the front needle, but this time leave the stitch on the left front needle and pull the yarn all the way through as before.
- Knit the first stitch on the back needle.
- Drop the stitch off the left back needle and pull the yarn all the way through.
- Purl the next stitch on the back needle.
- Leave this stitch on the left back needle and pull the yarn all the way through.

Repeat as set until two stitches remain, then work these two stitches together and drop both stitches off the needles. Pull the yarn all the way through and thread on a tapestry needle.
Bring yarn to the inside of work and weave in ends, tacking down the last loops as necessary for a neat finish.

Heels and toes

SHAPING THE TOE

There are many different ways of shaping a toe. This is the most common, and it is guaranteed to work!

Begin with 64 sts divided between three needles (32 sts on N1, 16 sts on N2 and 16 sts on N3).

Round 1: Work to last 3 stitches on N1, k2tog, k1; on N2 k1, skpo, work to last 3 sts, k2tog, k1, on N3 k1, skpo, work to end.

Round 2: K all sts.

Rep last two rounds until 40 sts rem (10/20/10) sts.

Next round: As round 1.

Rep until 20 sts rem (5/10/5) sts), then knit the 5 sts from N1 on to the end of N3 so you have (10 sts on each of two needles).

Using Kitchener Stitch, graft these stitches together.

WRAPPING STITCHES

A wrap stitch is used to eliminate the risk of holes when using the short row shaping method. Work to where the wrap is required; then to work it, slip the next stitch on to the right needle, bring the yarn to the front of work between the needles, and slip the same stitch back on to the left needle. On subsequent rows, work the loop and the wrapped stitch as k2tog and turn. Continue from pattern.

EASY HEEL EXPLAINED

This simple technique for heels works over any even number of stitches. The following example produces a heel suitable for an adult-size sock in standard 4-ply sock yarn.

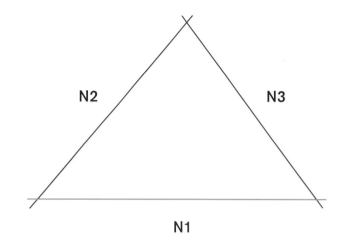

EXAMPLE

Cast on 64 stitches on 2.5mm needles. Work in rounds until the point where the heel is to begin, then divide stitches so that there are 32 on N1, 16 on N2 and 16 on N3. N1 holds the stitches for the top of the foot, while N1 and N3 hold the stitches that will form the heel.

To shape the heel, increase 1 st at the beginning of N2 and at the end of N3 on every alternate row. The diagram shows N1 as a green line, and N2 and N3 as red lines. The increase points are where N1 meets N2 and N3, or where the green line meets the red lines.

Note: the number of stitches on N2 and N3 increases from 16 to 30. The number of stitches on N1 remains constant at 32.

HEEL DECREASES

The stitches on N2 and N3 now need to be decreased to shape the heel, leaving 32 stitches on N1. To do this, work across to the last stitch on N1, then on N2 k1, k2tog, k1, turn. (32+1)

Next row: Sl1p-wise, p2 on N1, p across the 32 sts on N1, then on N3 p1, p2 tog, p1, turn.

Next row: Sl1, k2 on N3, k across 32 sts on N1, then on N2 k1, k2tog, k1, turn.

Cont as set, working back and forth in rows, until there are 16 sts on N2 and 16 sts on N3 (32 sts rem on N1).

Cont on these 64 sts down the length of the foot until it measures 3in (7.5cm) less than desired length for socks. Work toe as desired.

Note: the number of stitches on N2 and N3 increases from 16 to 30. The number of stitches on N1 remains constant at 32.

Conversions

UK/US YARN WEIGHTS

UK	US
2–ply	Lace
3–ply	Fingering
4–ply	Sport
Double knitting	Light worsted
Aran	Fisherman/worsted
Chunky	Bulky
Super chunky	Extra bulky

KNITTING NEEDLE SIZES

UK	METRIC	US
14	2mm	0
13	2.25mm	1
12	2.5mm	–
–	2.75mm	2
11	3mm	–
10	3.25mm	3
9	3.5mm	4
9	3.75mm	5
8	4mm	6
7	4.5mm	7
6	5mm	8
5	5.5mm	9
4	6mm	10
3	6.5mm	10.5
2	7mm	10.5
1	7.5mm	11
0	8mm	11
00	9mm	13
000	10mm	15

Abbreviations

approx	approximately
cont	continue
cm	centimetre(s)
dg-st	double garter stitch (2 rounds p, 2 rounds k)
DK	double knitting
foll	following
inc	increase by working twice into stitch
in	inch(es)
k	knit
k-wise	with needles positioned as for working a knit stitch
k2tog	knit two stitches together
M1L	make 1 stitch slanting to the left
M1R	make 1 stitch slanting to the right
p	purl
p2tog	purl two stitches together
p-wise	with needles positioned as for working a purl stitch
rem	remaining
rep	repeat
RS	right side of work
skpo	slip one, knit one, pass slipped stitch over
ssk	slip one stitch knitwise, then slip 1 st purl-wise, then knit the two stitches together through the back of the loops
ssp	slip one stitch k-wise, slip one stitch p-wise, then purl sts tog
st(s)	stitch(es)
*	work instructions following * , then repeat as directed
( )	repeat instructions inside brackets as directed
WS	wrong side of work
yf	yarn forward